God's Little Instruction Book for Teens

Honor Books
Tulsa, Oklahoma

God's Little Instruction Book for Teens
ISBN 1-56292-519-9
Copyright © 1998 by Honor Books
P.O. Box 55388
Tulsa, OK 74155

3rd Printing

Get "Fired Up"!

You haven't quite made it all the way into the world of adults, but you're almost there—and you sure aren't a kid anymore!

Lots of new issues and challenges face you every day. Where do you turn for advice? How do you get "fired up" when you're feeling a little knocked down?

God's Little Instruction Book for Teens is one great source of wisdom and encouragement to help you meet life head on—not just getting by, but with poise, style, integrity, and faith.

Take the powerful quotes and scriptures found in this handy little book to heart. You will be well on your way to making an incredible difference in your world!

When you were born, you cried and the world rejoiced. Live your life in such a manner that when you die the world cries and you rejoice.

The memory of the righteous will be a blessing.
— Proverbs 10:7 NIV

Many receive advice; only the wise profit by it.

Pride only breeds quarrels,
but wisdom is found in those who take advice.
— Proverbs 13:10 NIV

God's Little Instruction Book for Teens

The only way to have a friend is to be one.

A man that hath friends must shew himself friendly.
— Proverbs 18:24

The world wants your best, but God wants your all.

Thou shalt love the Lord thy God with all thy heart,
and with all thy soul, and with all thy mind.
— Matthew 22:37

God's Little Instruction Book for Teens

A Christian must keep the faith, but not to himself.

Go ye into all the world, and preach the gospel to every creature.
— Mark 16:15

No horse gets anywhere until he is harnessed. No life ever grows great until it is focused, dedicated, disciplined.

In a race, everyone runs but only one person gets first prize. . . .
To win the contest you must deny yourselves many things
that would keep you from doing your best.
— 1 Corinthians 9:24,25 TLB

9

I have never been hurt by anything I didn't say.

Don't talk so much. You keep putting your foot in your mouth.
Be sensible and turn off the flow!
— Proverbs 10:19 TLB

We too often love things and use people, when we should be using things and loving people.

Be devoted to one another in brotherly love.
Honor one another above yourselves.
— Romans 12:10 NIV

11

When you flee temptations, don't leave a forwarding address.

Now flee from youthful lusts, and pursue righteousness . . .
with those who call on the Lord from a pure heart.
— 2 Timothy 2:22 NAS

God's Little Instruction Book for Teens

Whatever you dislike in another person, take care to correct in yourself.

Why do you look at the speck of sawdust in your brother's eye
and pay no attention to the plank in your own eye?
— Matthew 7:3 NIV

God's Little Instruction Book for Teens

Shoot for the moon. Even if you miss it you will land among the stars.

Aim for perfection.
— 2 Corinthians 13:11 NIV

The secret of success is to do the common things uncommonly well.

Seest thou a man diligent in his business?
he shall stand before kings;
he shall not stand before mean men.
— Proverbs 22:29

God's Little Instruction Book for Teens

Definition of status: Buying something you don't need with money you don't have to impress people you don't like.

But they do all their deeds to be noticed by men.
— Matthew 23:5 NAS

I like the dreams of the future better than the history of the past.

Remember ye not the former things,
neither consider the things of old.
Behold, I will do a new thing.
— Isaiah 43:18,19

17

The way to get to the top is to get off your bottom.

How long will you lie down, O sluggard?
When will you arise from your sleep?
— Proverbs 6:9 NAS

You are only what you are when no one is looking.

Not with eyeservice, as menpleasers; but as the servants of Christ, doing the will of God from the heart.
— Ephesians 6:6

There are times when silence is golden, other times it is just plain yellow.

To every thing there is a season . . .
a time to keep silence, and a time to speak.
— Ecclesiastes 3:1,7

A true friend never gets in your way unless you happen to be going down.

If one falls down, his friend can help him up.
But pity the man who falls and has no one to help him up!
— Ecclesiastes 4:10 NIV

Every job is a self-portrait of the person who does it. Autograph your work with excellence.

Daniel was preferred above the presidents and princes, because an excellent spirit was in him.
— Daniel 6:3

God's Little Instruction Book for Teens

The best things in life are *not* free.

Forasmuch as ye know that ye were not redeemed with
corruptible things, as silver and gold . . . but with the precious
blood of Christ, as of a lamb without blemish and without spot.
— 1 Peter 1:18,19

23

God's Little Instruction Book for Teens

You can lead a boy to college, but you cannot make him think.

It is senseless to pay tuition to educate
a rebel who has no heart for truth.
— Proverbs 17:16 TLB

If a man cannot be a Christian in the place where he is, he cannot be a Christian anywhere.

Don't work hard only when your master is watching and then shirk when he isn't looking; work hard and with gladness all the time, as though working for Christ, doing the will of God with all your hearts.
— Ephesians 6:6,7 TLB

Don't ask God for what you think is good; ask Him for what He thinks is good for you.

After this manner therefore pray ye . . . Thy kingdom come.
Thy will be done in earth, as it is in heaven.
— Matthew 6:9,10

Opportunities are seldom labeled.

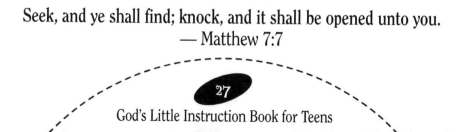

Seek, and ye shall find; knock, and it shall be opened unto you.
— Matthew 7:7

27

The wise does at once what the fool does at last.

He that gathereth in summer is a wise son:
but he that sleepeth in harvest is a son that causeth shame.
— Proverbs 10:5

Nothing great was ever achieved without enthusiasm.

The joy of the LORD is your strength.
— Nehemiah 8:10

God's Little Instruction Book for Teens

Trust in yourself and you are doomed to disappointment; but trust in God, and you are never to be confounded in time or eternity.

It is better to take refuge in the LORD than to trust in man.
— Psalm 118:8 NIV

Don't be discouraged; everyone who got where he is, started where he was.

Though your beginning was insignificant,
Yet your end will increase greatly.
— Job 8:7 NAS

31

God's Little Instruction Book for Teens

Maturity doesn't come with age; it comes with acceptance of responsibility.

When I was a child, I spake as a child, I understood as a child,
I thought as a child: but when I became a man,
I put away childish things.
— 1 Corinthians 13:11

The man who wins may have been counted out several times, but he didn't hear the referee.

For though a righteous man falls seven times, he rises again.
— Proverbs 24:16 NIV

33

The happiest people don't necessarily have the best of everything. They just make the best of everything.

For I have learned, in whatsoever state I am, therewith to be content. I can do all things through Christ which strengtheneth me.
— Philippians 4:11,13

Keep company with good men and good men you will imitate.

Iron sharpeneth iron; so a man sharpeneth
the countenance of his friend.
— Proverbs 27:17

God's Little Instruction Book for Teens

Learn by experience—preferably other people's.

All these things happened to them as examples—
as object lessons to us—to warn us against
doing the same things.
— 1 Corinthians 10:11 TLB

Many men have too much will power. It's *won't* power they lack.

A man without self-control is as defenseless
as a city with broken-down walls.
— Proverbs 25:28 TLB

God's Little Instruction Book for Teens

It's not hard to make decisions when you know what your values are.

But Daniel purposed in his heart that he would not defile himself.
— Daniel 1:8

Conquer yourself rather than the world.

Similarly, encourage the young men to be self-controlled.
— Titus 2:6 NIV

God's Little Instruction Book for Teens

I am only one, but still I am one.
I cannot do everything, but still
I can do something; I will not
refuse to do the something I can do.

Under his (Christ's) direction the whole body is fitted together
perfectly, and each part in its own special way helps the other parts.
— Ephesians 4:16 TLB

God's Little Instruction Book for Teens

Politeness goes far, yet costs nothing.

A kind man benefits himself.
— Proverbs 11:17 NIV

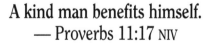

41

God's Little Instruction Book for Teens

We should behave to our friends as we would wish our friends to behave to us.

And as ye would that men should do to you,
do ye also to them likewise.
— Luke 6:31

Who ceases to be a friend, never was one.

This people honors Me with their lips,
but their heart is far away from Me.
— Mark 7:6 NAS

43

God's Little Instruction Book for Teens

Character is what you are in the dark.

The integrity of the upright shall guide them.
— Proverbs 11:3

Adversity causes some men to break; others to break records.

If thou faint in the day of adversity, thy strength is small.
— Proverbs 24:10

God's Little Instruction Book for Teens

Learn to say "No"; it will be of more use to you than to be able to read Latin.

Just say a simple yes or no, so that you will not sin.
— James 5:12 TLB

A man who wants to lead the orchestra must turn his back on the crowd.

Wherefore come out from among them, and be ye separate,
saith the Lord, and touch not the unclean thing; and I will receive you.
— 2 Corinthians 6:17

Men are alike in their promises. It is only in their deeds that they differ.

Many a man claims to have unfailing love,
but a faithful man who can find?
— Proverbs 20:6 NIV

Don't cross your bridges until you get to them. We spend our lives defeating ourselves crossing bridges we never get to.

So don't be anxious about tomorrow. God will take care of your tomorrow too. Live one day at a time.
— Matthew 6:34 TLB

He that has learned to obey will know how to command.

The wise in heart accept commands,
but a chattering fool comes to ruin.
— Proverbs 10:8 NIV

You must have long-range goals
to keep you from being frustrated
by short-range failures.

Let us fix our eyes on Jesus, the author and perfecter of our faith,
who for the joy set before him endured the cross, scorning its shame,
and sat down at the right hand of the throne of God.
— Hebrews 12:2 NIV

Clear your mind of can't.

I can do all things through Christ which strengtheneth me.
— Philippians 4:13

The future belongs to those who believe in the beauty of their dreams.

Anything is possible if you have faith.
— Mark 9:23 TLB

The future belongs to those who see possibilities before they become obvious.

For the vision is yet for an appointed time . . .
it will surely come, it will not tarry.
— Habakkuk 2:3

When I was a young man I observed that nine out of ten things I did were failures. I didn't want to be a failure, so I did ten times more work.

He becometh poor that dealeth with a slack hand:
but the hand of the diligent maketh rich.
— Proverbs 10:4

Luck is a matter of preparation meeting opportunity.

Make the most of every opportunity.
— Colossians 4:5 NIV

God's Little Instruction Book for Teens

Jumping to conclusions is not half as good an exercise as digging for facts.

Study to shew thyself approved unto God, a workman that needeth not to be ashamed, rightly dividing the word of truth.
— 2 Timothy 2:15

God's Little Instruction Book for Teens

The most valuable of all talents is that of never using two words when one will do.

In the multitude of words there wanteth not sin:
but he that refraineth his lips is wise.
— Proverbs 10:19

Laziness is often mistaken for patience.

Let us lay aside every weight, and the sin which doth so easily beset us,
and let us run with patience the race that is set before us.
— Hebrews 12:1

God's Little Instruction Book for Teens

One-half the trouble of this life can be traced to saying "yes" too quick, and not saying "no" soon enough.

Seest thou a man that is hasty in his words?
there is more hope of a fool than of him.
— Proverbs 29:20

God's Little Instruction Book for Teens

I would rather fail in the cause
that someday will triumph
than triumph in a cause
that someday will fail.

Now thanks be unto God, which always
causeth us to triumph in Christ.
— 2 Corinthians 2:14

Carve your name on hearts and not on marble.

The only letter I need is you yourselves!
They can see that you are a letter from Christ, written by us. . . .
not one carved on stone, but in human hearts.
— 2 Corinthians 3:2,3 TLB

A knowledge of the Bible without a college course is more valuable than a college course without the Bible.

All scripture is given by inspiration of God, and is profitable for doctrine, for reproof, for correction, for instruction in righteousness: that the man of God may be perfect, thoroughly furnished unto all good works.
— 2 Timothy 3:16,17

Little minds are tamed and subdued by misfortune; but great minds rise above them.

For a just man falleth seven times, and riseth up again.
— Proverbs 24:16

There is no poverty that can overtake diligence.

He becometh poor that dealeth with a slack hand:
but the hand of the diligent maketh rich.
— Proverbs 10:4

God's Little Instruction Book for Teens

Never despair; but if you do, work on in despair.

But as for you, be strong and do not give up,
for your work will be rewarded.
— 2 Chronicles 15:7 NIV

You can accomplish more in one hour with God than one lifetime without Him.

With God all things are possible.
— Matthew 19:26

If you don't stand for something, you'll fall for anything!

If you do not stand firm in your faith, you will not stand at all.
— Isaiah 7:9 NIV

The difference between ordinary and extraordinary is that little extra.

Whatsoever thy hand findeth to do, do it with thy might.
— Ecclesiastes 9:10

Man cannot discover new oceans unless he has the courage to lose sight of the shore.

Peter got out of the boat, and walked on the water
and came toward Jesus.
— Matthew 14:29 NAS

70

Fads come and go; wisdom and character go on forever.

O my son, be wise and stay in God's paths.
— Proverbs 23:19 TLB

Perseverance is a great element of success; if you only knock long enough and loud enough at the gate, you are sure to wake up somebody.

Ask, and it shall be given you; seek, and ye shall find; knock, and it shall be opened unto you.
— Luke 11:9

God's Little Instruction Book for Teens

Consider the postage stamp: its usefulness consists in the ability to stick to one thing till it gets there.

I have fought a good fight, I have finished my course, I have kept the faith.
— 2 Timothy 4:7

73

It needs more skill
than I can tell
To play the second
fiddle well.

But he that is greatest among you shall be your servant.
— Matthew 23:11

God's Little Instruction Book for Teens

A man never discloses his own character so clearly as when he describes another's.

A good man out of the good treasure of the heart
bringeth forth good things: and an evil man out of
the evil treasure bringeth forth evil things.
— Matthew 12:35

75

God's Little Instruction Book for Teens

The greatest use of life is to spend it for something that will outlast it.

But store up for yourselves treasures in heaven, where moth and rust do not destroy, and where thieves do not break in and steal.
— Matthew 6:20 NIV

Every man's work, whether it be literature, or music, or pictures, or architecture, or anything else, is always a portrait of himself.

As in water face reflects face, so the heart of man reflects man.
— Proverbs 27:19 NAS

What we do on some great occasion will probably depend on what we already are; and what we are will be the result of previous years of self-discipline.

But I keep under my body, and bring it into subjection.
— 1 Corinthians 9:27

God's Little Instruction Book for Teens

Our deeds determine us, as much as we determine our deeds.

Even a child is known by his actions,
by whether his conduct is pure and right.
— Proverbs 20:11 NIV

God's Little Instruction Book for Teens

What you do speaks so loud that I cannot hear what you say.

Show me your faith without deeds,
and I will show you my faith by what I do.
— James 2:18 NIV

God's Little Instruction Book for Teens

All virtue is summed up in dealing justly.

He hath shewed thee, O man, what is good;
and what doth the Lord require of thee, but to do justly,
and to love mercy, and to walk humbly with thy God?
— Micah 6:8

No matter what a man's past may have been, his future is spotless.

Forgetting those things which are behind,
and reaching forth unto those things which are before.
— Philippians 3:13

One of Life's great rules is this: The more you give, the more you get.

The liberal soul shall be made fat: and he that watereth shall be watered also himself.
— Proverbs 11:25

God's Little Instruction Book for Teens

Everything comes to him who hustles while he waits.

We do not want you to become lazy, but to imitate those who through faith and patience inherit what has been promised.
— Hebrews 6:12 NIV

A well-trained memory is one that permits you to forget everything that isn't worth remembering.

Finally, brethren, whatsoever things are true, whatsoever things are honest, whatsoever things are just . . . if there be any virtue, and if there be any praise, think on these things.
— Philippians 4:8

Defeat is not the worst of failures. Not to have tried is the true failure.

Be strong and of a good courage; be not afraid, neither be thou dismayed: for the LORD thy God is with thee whithersoever thou goest.

— Joshua 1:9

Unless you try to do something
beyond what you have
already mastered,
you will never grow.

Reaching forth unto those things which are before, I press toward
the mark for the prize of the high calling of God in Christ Jesus.
— Philippians 3:13,14

I don't know the secret to success, but the key to failure is to try to please everyone.

Am I now trying to win the approval of men, or of God?
— Galatians 1:10 NIV

Kites rise highest against the wind, not with it.

For when the way is rough, your patience has a chance to grow.
So let it grow, and don't try to squirm out of your problems.
— James 1:3,4 TLB

God's Little Instruction Book for Teens

The secret of success is to be like a duck—smooth and unruffled on top, but paddling furiously underneath.

But I laboured more abundantly than they all:
yet not I, but the grace of God which was with me.
— 1 Corinthians 15:10

The cheerful man will do more in the same time, will do it better, will preserve it longer, than the sad or sullen.

When a man is gloomy, everything seems to go wrong;
when he is cheerful, everything seems right!
— Proverbs 15:15 TLB

God's Little Instruction Book for Teens

Money is a good servant but a bad master.

The rich ruleth over the poor, and
the borrower is servant to the lender.
— Proverbs 22:7

No plan is worth the paper it is printed on unless it starts you doing something.

But be ye doers of the word, and not hearers only,
deceiving your own selves.
— James 1:22

God's Little Instruction Book for Teens

Life is a coin. You can spend it any way you wish, but you can spend it only once.

And as it is appointed unto men once to die,
but after this the judgment.
— Hebrews 9:27

Only passions, great passions, can elevate the soul to great things.

Fervent in spirit; serving the Lord.
— Romans 12:11

God's Little Instruction Book for Teens

Failures want pleasing methods, successes want pleasing results.

No discipline seems pleasant at the time, but painful.
Later on, however, it produces a harvest of righteousness
and peace for those who have been trained by it.
— Hebrews 12:11 NIV

Once a word has been allowed to escape, it cannot be recalled.

Let no corrupt communication proceed out of your mouth,
but that which is good to the use of edifying,
that it may minister grace unto the hearers.
— Ephesians 4:29

Most of the things worth doing in the world had been declared impossible before they were done.

But with God all things are possible.
— Matthew 19:26

God's Little Instruction Book for Teens

Obstacles are those frightful things you see when you take your eyes off the goal.

So Peter . . . walked on the water toward Jesus. But when he looked around at the high waves, he was terrified and began to sink.
Matthew 14:29,30 TLB

God's Little Instruction Book for Teens

A good reputation is more valuable than money.

A good name is rather to be chosen than great riches.
— Proverbs 22:1

An error doesn't become a mistake until you refuse to correct it.

He who heeds discipline shows the way to life,
but whoever ignores correction leads others astray.
— Proverbs 10:17 NIV

Hating people is like burning down your own house to get rid of a rat.

But if ye bite and devour one another,
take heed that ye be not consumed one of another.
— Galatians 5:15

God's Little Instruction Book for Teens

Laughter is the sun that drives winter from the human face.

A merry heart maketh a cheerful countenance:
but by sorrow of the heart the spirit is broken.
— Proverbs 15:13

103

Good nature begets smiles, smiles beget friends, and friends are better than a fortune.

The light in the eyes [of him whose heart is joyful]
rejoices the heart of others.
— Proverbs 15:30 AMP

No person was ever honored for what he received. Honor has been the reward for what he gave.

The righteous give without sparing.
— Proverbs 21:26 NIV

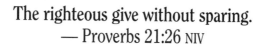

105

The difference between the right word and the almost right word is the difference between lightning and the lightning bug.

A word fitly spoken is like apples of gold in pictures of silver.
— Proverbs 25:11

This world belongs to the man who is wise enough to change his mind in the presence of facts.

Whoever heeds correction gains understanding.
— Proverbs 15:32 NIV

107

Do not remove a fly from your friend's forehead with a hatchet.

Reprove, rebuke, exhort, with great patience and instruction.
— 2 Timothy 4:2 NAS

God's Little Instruction Book for Teens

Every calling is great when greatly pursued.

I press toward the mark for the prize of
the high calling of God in Christ Jesus.
— Philippians 3:14

God's Little Instruction Book for Teens

Treat everybody alike, no matter from what station in life he comes . . . really great men and women are those who are natural, frank, and honest with everyone with whom they come into contact.

Don't show favoritism.
— James 2:1 NIV

'Tis better to be alone, than in bad company.

Do not be misled: "Bad company corrupts good character."
— 1 Corinthians 15:33 NIV

God's Little Instruction Book for Teens

The rotten apple spoils his companion.

He that walketh with wise men shall be wise:
but a companion of fools shall be destroyed.
— Proverbs 13:20

Patience is bitter but its fruit is sweet.

For ye have need of patience, that, after ye have done
the will of God, ye might receive the promise.
— Hebrews 10:36

Motivation is when your dreams put on work clothes.

Whatever you do, work at it with all your heart,
as working for the Lord, not for men.
— Colossians 3:23 NIV

Not only to say the right thing
in the right place, but far more
difficult, to leave unsaid the wrong
thing at the tempting moment.

Self-control means controlling the tongue!
A quick retort can ruin everything.
— Proverbs 13:3 TLB

God's Little Instruction Book for Teens

School seeks to get you ready for examination; life gives the finals.

Examine yourselves to see whether
you are in the faith; test yourselves.
— 2 Corinthians 13:5 NIV

116

God's Little Instruction Book for Teens

Diligence is the mother of good fortune.

The plans of the diligent lead to profit.
— Proverbs 21:5 NIV

The road to success is dotted with many tempting parking places.

Let us lay aside every weight, and the sin which doth so easily
beset us, and let us run with patience the race that is set before us.
— Hebrews 12:1

When you are laboring for others
let it be with the same zeal
as if it were for yourself.

Each of you should look not only to your own interests,
but also to the interests of others.
— Philippians 2:4 NIV

God's Little Instruction Book for Teens

The Bible knows nothing of a hierarchy of labor. No work is degrading. If it ought to be done, then it is good work.

To rejoice in his labour; this is the gift of God.
— Ecclesiastes 5:19

The ripest peach is highest on the tree.

Let us not become weary in doing good, for at the proper time we will reap a harvest if we do not give up.
— Galatians 6:9 NIV

When you do the things you have to do
when you have to do them, the day will come
when you can do the things you want to do
when you want to do them.

He becometh poor that dealeth with a slack hand:
but the hand of the diligent maketh rich.
— Proverbs 10:4

A man without mirth is like
a wagon without springs,
he is jolted disagreeably by
every pebble in the road.

A merry heart doeth good like a medicine:
but a broken spirit drieth the bones.
— Proverbs 17:22

The two most important words: "Thank you." The most important word: "We." The least important word: "I."

Don't be selfish. . . . Be humble, thinking of
others as better than yourself.
— Philippians 2:3 TLB

Here's the key to success and the key to failure: we become what we think about.

Finally, brethren, whatsoever things are true,
whatsoever things are honest . . . if there be any virtue,
and if there be any praise, think on these things.
— Philippians 4:8

125

Always bear in mind that your own resolution to success is more important than any other one thing.

For the Lord God will help me; therefore shall I not be confounded: therefore have I set my face like a flint, and I know that I shall not be ashamed.

— Isaiah 50:7

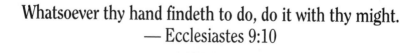

Triumph is just "umph" added to try.

Whatsoever thy hand findeth to do, do it with thy might.
— Ecclesiastes 9:10

God's Little Instruction Book for Teens

A goal properly set is halfway reached.

And the LORD answered me, and said, Write the vision,
and make it plain upon tables, that he may run that readeth it.
— Habakkuk 2:2

God's Little Instruction Book for Teens

I think the one lesson I have
learned is that there is no
substitute for paying attention.

Therefore we ought to give the more earnest heed to the things
which we have heard, lest at any time we should let them slip.
— Hebrews 2:1

God's Little Instruction Book for Teens

A good listener is not only popular everywhere, but after a while he knows something.

The ear that heareth the reproof of life abideth among the wise.
— Proverbs 15:31

God's Little Instruction Book for Teens

You may be disappointed if you fail, but you are doomed if you don't try.

The sluggard craves and gets nothing, but the desires of the diligent are fully satisfied.
— Proverbs 13:4 NIV

God's Little Instruction Book for Teens

Success is never final; failure is never fatal; it is courage that counts.

Be of good courage, and he shall strengthen
your heart, all ye that hope in the LORD.
— Psalm 31:24

I count him braver who overcomes his desires than him who conquers his enemies; for the hardest victory is the victory over self.

I beat my body and make it my slave.
— 1 Corinthians 9:27 NIV

God's Little Instruction Book for Teens

Vision is the world's
most desperate need.
There are no hopeless situations,
only people who think hopelessly.

Where there is no vision, the people perish.
— Proverbs 29:18

People are lonely because they build walls instead of bridges.

You should be like one big happy family . . . loving one another
with tender hearts and humble minds.
— 1 Peter 3:8 TLB

Forgiveness means giving up your right to punish another.

And when you stand praying, if you hold anything against anyone,
forgive him, so that your Father in heaven may forgive you your sins.
— Mark 11:25 NIV

The most important single ingredient in the formula of success is knowing how to get along with people.

See that no one pays back evil for evil, but always try
to do good to each other and to everyone else.
— 1 Thessalonians 5:15 TLB

Everyone thinks of changing the world, but no one thinks of changing himself.

Unless you change and become like little children, you will never enter the kingdom of heaven.
— Matthew 18:3 NIV

Courage is resistance to fear, mastery of fear— not absence of fear.

Yea, though I walk through the valley of the shadow of death, I will fear no evil: for thou art with me; thy rod and thy staff they comfort me.
— Psalm 23:4

Prayer is an invisible tool which is wielded in a visible world.

For the weapons of our warfare are not carnal, but mighty through God to the pulling down of strong holds.
— 2 Corinthians 10:4

Money is like an arm or leg: use it or lose it.

For to him who has will more be given . . .
and he will have great plenty; but from him who has not,
even the little he has will be taken away.
— Matthew 13:12 TLB

God's Little Instruction Book for Teens

In trying times, don't quit trying.

The righteous also shall hold on his way, and he
that hath clean hands shall be stronger and stronger.
— Job 17:9

Let us not say, "Every man is the architect of his own fortune;" but let us say, "Every man is the architect of his own character."

Till I die I will not remove mine integrity from me.
My righteousness I hold fast, and will not let it go:
my heart shall not reproach me so long as I live.
— Job 27:5,6

143

It is impossible for that man to despair who remembers that his Helper is omnipotent.

I will lift up my eyes to the mountains; from whence shall my help come? My help comes from the LORD, who made heaven and earth.
— Psalm 121:1,2 NAS

Service is nothing but love in work clothes.

The more lowly your service to others, the greater you are.
To be the greatest, be a servant.
— Matthew 23:11 TLB

Those that have done nothing in life are not qualified to judge of those that have done little.

Judge not, and ye shall not be judged: condemn not, and ye shall not be condemned.
— Luke 6:37

People, places, and things were never meant to give us life. God alone is the author of a fulfilling life.

I am come that they might have life, and that they might have it more abundantly.
— John 10:10

COMMON COURTESIES
FOR TEENS
SECTION

Always say "thank you" when you
receive a favor, and say "excuse me"
or "pardon me" when needing to
interrupt a discussion.

And just as you want people to treat you, treat them in the same way.
— Luke 6:31 NAS

God's Little Instruction Book for Teens

Always knock and ask permission before entering someone's room.

So then, while we have opportunity, let us do good to all men.
— Galatians 6:10 NAS

Don't put your feet up on furniture.
Feet do not enhance the look of
the desk or the table.

And just as you want people to treat you, treat them in the same way.
— Luke 6:31 NAS

Always RSVP promptly to every invitation you receive.

So then, while we have opportunity, let us do good to all men.
— Galatians 6:10 NAS

Return anything borrowed on time, and in good or better condition than received.

And just as you want people to treat you, treat them in the same way.
— Luke 6:31 NAS

Be on time for appointments;
leave on time, too, for nothing is
more boring than someone who
overstays his welcome.

So then, while we have opportunity, let us do good to all men.
— Galatians 6:10 NAS

When you dial a wrong number,
say, "I'm sorry, excuse me"—
instead of slamming down the
receiver in the other person's ear.

And just as you want people to treat you, treat them in the same way.
— Luke 6:31 NAS

157

Acknowledgments

The publisher would like to honor and acknowledge the following, for the quotes used in this book:
Publius Syrus (7,102), R. W. Emerson (8,31,82), Jim Patrick (10), H. E. Fosdick (11,104), Calvin Coolidge (12,107), Sprat (15), Les Brown (16), John Rockefeller, Jr. (17), Dr. Eugene Swearingen (18,20), Thomas Jefferson (19,60), Robert C. Edward (21), Ed Cole (22,34,142), Arnold Glasow (23), Kin Hubbard (26), Henry Ward Beecher (27,125), John A. Shedd (29,39), Dwight L. Moody (32,46), H. E. Jansen (35), Roy Disney (40), Descartes (41), Helen Keller (42), Seneca (43), Aristotle (44,83,135), William A. Ward (47), Charles H. Spurgeon (48,64), Moliere (50), Bob Bales (51), Solon (52), Charles C. Noble (53), Samuel Johnson (54,148), Eleanor Roosevelt (55), John Sculley (56), George Bernard Shaw (57), Oprah Winfrey (58), Benjamin Franklin (62,114), Woodrow Wilson (63), William Lyon Phelps (65), Washington Irving (66), Terence (68), Henry Wadsworth Longfellow (74), Josh Billings (75), Jean Paul Richter (77), William James (78), Samuel Butler (79), H. P. Liddon (80), George Elliot (80), John R. Rice (84), William H. Danforth (85,95,112), Thomas Edison (86), Orlando Battista (87,103), George Woodberry (88), Ronald E. Osborn (89), Bill Cosby (90), Winston Churchill (91,134), Thomas Carlyle (93), Bacon (94), Lillian Dickson (94), Denis Diderot (97), Earl Nightingale (98,127), Horace (99), Louis D. Brandeis (100), Hannah More (101), Victor Hugo (105), David Dunn (106), Mark Twain (108,141), Roy L. Smith (109), Chinese Proverb (110), Oliver Wendell Holmes (111), George Washington (113), Parks Robinson (116), George Sala (117), Say (118), Cervantes (119), Ben Patterson (122), James Riley (123), Zig Ziglar (124,130), Abraham Lincoln (128), Diane Sawyer (131), Wilson Mizner (132), Beverly Sills (133), Winefred Newman (136), Joseph Newton (137), Dennis Rainey (138), Theodore Roosevelt (139), Leo Tolstoy (140), Henry Ford (143), George Boardman (145), Jeremy Taylor (146), Gary Smalley & John Trent (149)

Additional copies of this book and other titles in the *God's Little Instruction Book* series are available from your local bookstore.

God's Little Instruction Book
God's Little Instruction Book II
God's Little Instruction Book III
God's Little Instruction Book for Dad
God's Little Instruction Book for Mom
God's Little Instruction Book for Couples
God's Little Instruction Book for Kids
God's Little Instruction Book for Kids II

Honor Books
Tulsa, Oklahoma